Embraced by God

Studies on God's Love

Based on *When God Whispers Your Name*

Max Lucado

General Editor

Contents

Introduction

When you meet your Father in heaven, he'll call your name. After all, your name is written on God's hand (Isaiah 49:16). What a remarkable thought! The King of heaven calling your name!

Not only does God know you, he wants you to fully experience life with him—his joy, his grace, his protection, and his presence.

Come along with me as we explore a life embraced by the God who whispers your name.

—Max Lucado

Jesus Parties

"Where did we get the notion that a good Christian is a solemn Christian? Who started the rumor that the sign of a disciple is a long face? How did we create this idea that the truly gifted are the heavy-hearted?"

—Max Lucado

1. Describe a time when you laughed until your sides hurt.

_____

_____

_____

_____

_____

_____

_____

_____

1

A Moment with Max

Max shares these insights with us in his book *When God Whispers Your Name*.

Why would Jesus, on his first journey, take his followers to a party? Didn't they have work to do? Didn't he have principles to teach? Wasn't his time limited? How could a wedding fit with his purpose on earth?

Why did Jesus go to the wedding?

I think Jesus went to the wedding to have fun.

Jesus went to the wedding because he liked the people, he liked the food, and heaven forbid, he may have even wanted to swirl the bride around the dance floor a time or two.

I'm not talking debauchery, drunkenness, and adultery. I'm not endorsing compromise, coarseness, or obscenity. I am simply crusading for the freedom to enjoy a good joke, enliven a dull party, and appreciate a fun evening.

Maybe these thoughts catch you by surprise. They do me. It's been awhile since I pegged Jesus as a party-lover. But he was. His foes accused him of eating too much, drinking too much, and hanging out with the wrong people! (See Matthew 11:19) I must confess: It's been awhile since I've been accused of having too much fun. How about you?

We used to be good at it. What has happened to us? What happened to clean joy and loud laughter? Is it our neckties that choke us? Is it our diplomas that dignify us? Is it the pew that stiffens us?

2. What most often keeps you from relaxing and having a good time?

_____

_____

_____

_____

_____

_____

3. If we fail to let go and have a good time every so often, how does that affect our attitude about life?

_____

_____

_____

_____

_____

_____

A Message from the Word

[18]I have seen what is best for people here on earth. They should eat and drink and enjoy their work, because the life God has given them on earth is short. [19]God gives some people the ability to enjoy the wealth and property he gives them, as well as the ability to accept their state in life and enjoy their work. [20]They do not worry about how short life is, because God keeps them busy with what they love to do.

Ecclesiastes 5:18-20

4. What does accepting our state in life have to do with being joyful?

_____

_____

_____

_____

_____

5. Why is it difficult for some people to be joyful?

_____

_____

_____

_____

6. What hinders some people from enjoying everything good that God has given them?

_____

_____

_____

_____

_____

_____

_____

More from the Word

[22]But the Spirit produces the fruit of love, joy, peace, patience, kindness, goodness, faithfulness, [23]gentleness, self-control. There is no law that says these things are wrong.

Galatians 5:22-23

7. What does enjoying life have to do with living according to the Spirit?

_____

_____

_____

_____

_____

_____

_____

8. What three answers first come to your mind in response to the question, "What do you have to be happy about?"

_____

_____

_____

_____

_____

_____

9. Think of someone who seems to have a good time in almost any circumstance. What do you think is that person's secret?

_____

_____

_____

_____

_____

_____

My Reflections

"Be a child again. Flirt. Giggle. Dip your cookie in your milk. Take a nap. Say you're sorry if you hurt someone. Chase a butterfly… Loosen up. Don't you have some people to hug, rocks to skip, or lips to kiss? Let someone else run the world for a while. Jesus took time for a party…shouldn't we?"

—Max

Journal

What is one fun, carefree activity I can enjoy today?

For Further Study

To study more about joy in the Lord, read Nehemiah 8:7-12; Psalm 19:8; Psalm 30:11-12; Psalm 68:3; Ecclesiastes 8:15; Matthew 11:19; John 15:9-12.

Additional Questions

10. How regularly do you think Jesus relaxed and laughed with his disciples?

_____

_____

_____

_____

_____

_____

11. When has a good laugh changed your outlook?

_____

_____

_____

_____

_____

_____

12. In what place or situation do you feel most relaxed and able to enjoy yourself? Why?

_____

_____

_____

_____

_____

Additional Thoughts

_____

_____

_____

_____

_____

_____

_____

_____

_____

_____

_____

_____

Hidden Heroes

*"**D**o heroes know when they are heroic?
Rarely. Are historic moments acknowledged
when they happen? You know the answer to
that one. (If not, a visit to the manger will
remind you.)"* —Max Lucado

1. Name one moment that we now consider historic that may have seemed like "just another day" to the people involved.

_____

_____

_____

_____

_____

_____

_____

A Moment with Max

Max shares these insights with us in his book *When God Whispers Your Name*.

A hero could be next door and you wouldn't know it. The fellow who changes the oil in your car could be one. A hero in coveralls? Maybe. Maybe as he works he prays, asking God to do with the heart of the driver what he does with the engine.

The day-care worker where you drop off the kids? Perhaps…

The parole officer downtown? Could be…

I know, I know. These folks don't fit our image of a hero. They look too, too,…well, normal. Give us four stars, titles, and headlines. But something tells me that for every hero in the spotlight, there are dozens in the shadows. They don't get press. They don't draw crowds. They don't even write books!

But behind every avalanche is a snowflake.

Behind a rock slide is a pebble.

An atomic explosion begins with one atom.

And a revival can begin with one sermon.

2. Describe an unsung hero in your life.

_____

_____

_____

_____

_____

3. What are some characteristics of an unsung hero?

_____

_____

_____

_____

A Message from the Word

[6]I planted the seed, and Apollos watered it. But God is the One who made it grow. [7]So the one who plants is not important, and the one who waters is not important. Only God, who makes things grow, is important. [8]The one who plants and the one who waters have the same purpose, and each will be rewarded for his own work. [9]We are God's workers, working together; you are like God's farm, God's house.

[10]Using the gift God gave me, I laid the foundation of that house like an expert builder. Others are building on that foundation, but all people should be careful how they build on it. [11]The foundation that has already been laid is Jesus Christ, and no one can lay down any other foundation.

1 Corinthians 3:6-11

4. Who are the people in your life who laid the foundation on which your faith is built?

_____

_____

_____

_____

_____

5. In what ways can we "plant" and "water" seeds of faith in others?

_____

_____

_____

_____

_____

_____

6. Why is it important to remember that only God can make things grow?

_____

_____

_____

_____

_____

_____

More from the Word

14 [28]We know that in everything God works for the good of those who love him. They are the people he called, because that was his plan. [29]God knew them before he made the world, and he decided that they would be like his Son so that Jesus would be the firstborn of many brothers. [30]God planned for them to be like his Son; and those he planned to be like his Son, he also called; and those he called, he also made right with him; and those he made right, he also glorified.

Romans 8:28-30

7. How does God go about making us like Jesus?

_____

_____

_____

_____

_____

_____

8. In what circumstances is it difficult to believe that God works for the good of those who love him?

_____

_____

_____

_____

_____

_____

9. When has a friend inspired or encouraged you to trust in God to work out the details of your life?

_____

_____ 15

_____

_____

_____

_____

My Reflections

"We seldom see history in the making, and we seldom recognize heroes. Which is just as well, for if we knew either, we might mess up both. But we'd do well to keep our eyes open. Tomorrow's Spurgeon might be mowing your lawn. And the hero who inspires him might be nearer than you think. He might be in your mirror." —Max

Journal

What good work has God accomplished through me recently?

For Further Study

To study more about God's work in our lives, read Psalm 138:7–8; Romans 9:16–18, 20–21; 2 Corinthians 5:1–5; 2 Timothy 1:8–9; 2 Timothy 2:20–21; Hebrews 6:16–20.

Additional Questions

10. When you were a child, how did you imagine a hero looked?

_____

_____

_____

_____

_____

11. When your life is over and you stand before God, what do you hope he will say to you?

_____

_____

_____

_____

_____

12. How does it feel to know that the Creator of the universe takes the time to work in your life each day?

_____

_____

_____

_____

_____

_____

Additional Thoughts

_____

_____

_____

_____

_____

_____

_____

_____

_____

The Voice of God

"Who knows? If the Bible were being written today, that might be your name in the eighth chapter of Acts." —Max Lucado

1. To what Bible character do you most relate and why?

_____

_____

_____

_____

_____

_____

_____

A Moment with Max

Max shares these insights with us in his book *When God Whispers Your Name*.

"An angel of the Lord said to Philip, 'Get ready and go south....' So Philip got ready and went" (Acts 8:26–27).

"The Spirit said to Philip, 'Go to that chariot and stay near it.' So...Philip ran toward the chariot" (Acts 8:29–30).

...Our typical response when we read these verses is to think Philip was a special guy. He had access to the Oval Office. He carried a first-century pager that God doesn't pass out anymore.

But don't be too quick...

"The true children of God are those who let God's Spirit lead them" (Romans 8:14).

...The Holy Spirit is the presence of God in our lives, carrying on the work of Jesus....In evangelism the Holy Spirit is on center stage. If the disciple teaches, it is because the Spirit teaches the disciple (Luke 12:12). If the listener is convicted, it is because the Spirit has penetrated (John 16:10). If the listener is converted, it is by the transforming power of the Spirit (Romans 8:11). If the new believer matures, it is because the Spirit makes him or her competent (2 Corinthians 3:6)

22

...You have the same Spirit working with you that Philip did. Some of you don't believe me. You're still cautious. I can hear you mumbling under your breath as you read, "Philip had something I don't. I've never heard an angel's voice." To which I counter, "How do you know Philip did?"

...Could it be that the angel's voice was every bit as miraculous as the one you and I hear?

2. What difference does it make in your life to know that the same Spirit guides you that guided Philip?

_____

_____

_____

_____

3. What factors sometime keep us from hearing the voice of God's Spirit?

_____

_____

_____

_____

_____

A Message from the Word

⁴There are different kinds of gifts, but they are all from the same Spirit. ⁵There are different ways to serve but the same Lord to serve. ⁶And there are different ways that God works through people but the same God. God works in all of us in everything we do. ⁷Something from the Spirit can be seen in each person, for the common good. ⁸The Spirit gives one person the ability to speak with wisdom, and the same Spirit gives another the ability to speak with knowledge. ⁹The same Spirit gives faith to one person. And, to another, that one Spirit gives gifts of healing. ¹⁰The Spirit gives to another person the power to do miracles, to another the ability to prophesy. And he gives to another the ability to know the difference between good and evil spirits. The Spirit gives one person the ability to speak in different kinds of languages and to another the ability to interpret those languages. ¹¹One Spirit, the same Spirit, does all these things, and the Spirit decides what to give each person.

¹²A person's body is only one thing, but it has many parts. Though there are many parts to a body, all those parts make only one body. Christ is like that also. ¹³Some of us are Jews, and some are Greeks. Some of us are slaves, and some are free. But we were all baptized into one body through one Spirit. And we were all made to share in the one Spirit.

1 Corinthians 12:4-13

4. What abilities has God given you for the common good of the church?

_____

_____

_____

_____

5. When is it most obvious to you that God's Spirit is influencing you?

_____

_____

_____

_____

6. How can we become more receptive to God's Spirit on a day-to-day basis?

_____

_____

_____

_____

_____

More from the Word

¹³If you use your lives to do the wrong things your sinful selves want, you will die spiritually. But if you use the Spirit's help to stop doing the wrong things you do with your body, you will have true life.

¹⁴The true children of God are those who let God's Spirit lead them. ¹⁵The Spirit we received does not make us slaves again to fear; it makes us children of God. With that Spirit we cry out, "Father." ¹⁶And the Spirit himself joins with our spirits to say we are God's children. ¹⁷If we are God's children, we will receive blessings from God together with Christ. But we must suffer as Christ suffered so that we will have glory as Christ has glory.

Romans 8:13–17

7. How is it comforting and challenging to know that God's Spirit lives in us?

_____

_____

_____

_____

_____

8. What part does the Holy Spirit play in our battle with our sinful nature?

_____

_____

_____

_____

_____

9. In what practical ways can we let God's Spirit lead us?

_____

_____

_____

_____

My Reflections

"You've heard the voice whispering your name, haven't you? You've felt the nudge to go and sensed the urge to speak. Hasn't it occurred to you? So, the next time you need to rest, go ahead. He'll keep you headed in the right direction. And the next time you make progress—thank him. He's the one providing the power." —Max

Journal

Holy Spirit, I need you in my life because…

_____

_____

_____

_____

_____

_____

_____

_____

_____

_____

_____

_____

_____

_____

_____

_____

For Further Study

To study more about the Holy Spirit, read John 4:24; John 14:26; Acts 2:2–4; Romans 8:26–29; 1 Corinthians 3:16–17; 1 Corinthians 14:14–16; 2 Corinthians 1:21–22; 2 Corinthians 3:17–18; 2 Corinthians 5:1–5; Galatians 5:16–18.

Additional Questions

10. When you feel urged to do something, how can you know if it is God's Spirit guiding you?

_____

_____

_____

_____

_____

_____

11. What did God do in Bible times that we don't expect him to do today?

_____

_____

_____

_____

_____

_____

_____

12. What are some concrete ways you have seen God work in people's lives today?

_____

_____

_____

_____

_____

_____

Additional Thoughts

_____

_____

_____

_____

_____

_____

_____

_____

_____

_____

Surprised by Grace

"I've never been surprised by God's judgment, but I'm still stunned by his grace....When we get to heaven, we'll be surprised at some of the folks we see. And some of them will be surprised when they see us." —Max Lucado

1. Describe a person in your life who has shown you the grace of God in a practical way.

_____

_____

_____

_____

_____

_____

_____

_____

A Moment with Max

Max shares these insights with us in his book *When God Whispers Your Name*.

God's judgment has never been a problem for me. In fact, it always seemed right. Lightning bolts on Sodom. Fire on Gomorrah. *Good job, God.* Egyptians swallowed in the Red Sea. *They had it coming.* Forty years of wandering to loosen the stiff necks of the Israelites? *Would've done it myself.* Ananias and Sapphira? *You bet.*

Discipline is easy for me to swallow. Logical to assimilate. Manageable and appropriate.

But God's grace? Anything but.

Examples? How much time do you have?

David the psalmist becomes David the voyeur, but by God's grace becomes David the psalmist again.

Peter denied Christ before he preached Christ.

Zacchaeus, the crook. The cleanest part of his life was the money he'd laundered. But Jesus still had time for him.

The thief on the cross: hellbent and hung-out-to-die one minute, heaven-bound and smiling the next.

Story after story. Prayer after prayer. Surprise after surprise.

32

2. Why is it easier to show judgment than grace to others?

_____

_____

_____

_____

_____

3. What is our motivation for showing grace to the people around us?

_____

_____

_____

_____

_____

A Message from the Word

³In the past we also were foolish. We did not obey, we were wrong, and we were slaves to many things our bodies wanted and enjoyed. We spent our lives doing evil and being jealous. People hated us, and we hated each other. ⁴But when the kindness and love of God our Savior was shown, ⁵he saved us because of his mercy. It was not because of good deeds we did to be right with him. He saved us through the washing that made us new people through the Holy Spirit. ⁶God poured out richly upon us that Holy Spirit through Jesus Christ our Savior. ⁷Being made right with God by his grace, we could have the hope of receiving the life that never ends.

⁸This teaching is true, and I want you to be sure the people understand these things. Then those who believe in God will be careful to use their lives for doing good. These things are good and will help everyone.

Titus 3:3-8

4. Why do we tend to forget what God saved us from?

_____

_____

_____

_____

_____

5. In what ways is our salvation an act of generosity on God's part?

_____

_____

_____

_____

6. How can we show to others even a shadow of the mercy and grace we've received from God?

_____

_____

_____

_____

_____

_____

More from the Word

34 ⁴But God's mercy is great, and he loved us very much. ⁵Though we were spiritually dead because of the things we did against God, he gave us new life with Christ. You have been saved by God's grace. ⁶And he raised us up with Christ and gave us a seat with him in the heavens. He did this for those in Christ Jesus ⁷so that for all future time he could show the very great riches of his grace by being kind to us in Christ Jesus. ⁸I mean that you have been saved by grace through believing. You did not save yourselves; it was a gift from God. ⁹It was not the result of your own efforts, so you cannot brag about it. ¹⁰God has made us what we are. In Christ Jesus, God made us to do good works, which God planned in advance for us to live our lives doing.

Ephesians 2:4-10

7. What three words best describe God's love for you?

_____

_____

_____

_____

_____

_____

_____

8. How would you describe God's mercy to a young child?

_____

_____

_____

_____

_____

_____

9. Having received God's love and mercy, why is it still difficult at times to show love and mercy to the people around us?

_____

_____

_____

_____

_____

My Reflections

"If God can tolerate my mistakes, can't I tolerate the mistakes of others? If God can overlook my errors, can't I overlook the errors of others? If God allows me with my foibles and failures to call him *Father,* shouldn't I extend the same grace to others?" —Max

Journal

To whom do I need to show God's grace this week? How?

For Further Study

To study more about grace, read John 1:14-17; Acts 15:7-11; Romans 3:21-26; Romans 5:20-21; 2 Corinthians 8:9; 2 Corinthians 12:9; Ephesians 2:4-5.

Additional Questions

10. Why do we get a sense of satisfaction when somebody gets what's coming to them?

_____

_____

_____

_____

_____

_____

11. Describe a world where everyone gives someone else the break they hope to receive.

_____

_____

_____

_____

_____

_____

_____

12. Is it possible to give too much grace? Explain your reasoning.

_____

_____

_____

_____

_____

_____

Additional Thoughts

_____

_____

_____

_____

_____

_____

_____

_____

_____

_____

What Is Your Price?

"God's foremost rule of finance is: We own nothing. We are managers, not owners. Stewards, not landlords. Maintenance people, not proprietors. Our money is not ours; it is his."
—*Max Lucado*

1. What purchase did you feel good about making long after the initial "thrill of the buy" wore off?

_____

_____

_____

_____

_____

_____

_____

_____

A Moment with Max

Max shares these insights with us in his book *When God Whispers Your Name*.

If money is the gauge of the heart, then this study revealed that money is on the heart of most Americans. In exchange for ten million dollars:

25 percent would abandon their family.

25 percent would abandon their church.

23 percent would become a prostitute for a week.

16 percent would give up their American citizenship.

16 percent would leave their spouse.

13 percent would put their children up for adoption.

Even more revealing than what Americans would do for ten million dollars is that most would do *something*. Two-thirds of those polled would agree to at least one—some to several—of the options...

Jesus had a word for that: *greed*.

Jesus also had a definition for greed. He called it the practice of measuring life by possessions.

Greed equates a person's worth with a person's purse.

You got a lot = you are a lot.

You got a little = you are little.

The consequence of such a philosophy is predictable. If you are the sum of what you own, then by all means own it all. No price is too high. No payment is too much.

2. What is your definition of greed?

_____

_____

_____

_____

3. Why does money tempt us to do things we wouldn't do for any other motivation?

_____

_____

_____

_____

A Message from the Word

[15]Then Jesus said to them, "Be careful and guard against all kinds of greed. Life is not measured by how much one owns."

[16]Then Jesus told this story: "There was a rich man who had some land, which grew a good crop. [17]He thought to himself, 'What will I do? I have no place to keep all my crops?' [18]Then he said, 'This is what I will do: I will tear down my barns and build bigger ones, and there I will store all my grain and other goods. [19]Then I can say to myself, "I have enough good things stored to last for many years. Rest, eat, drink, and enjoy life!"

[20]"But God said to him, 'Foolish man! Tonight your life will be taken from you. So who will get those things you have prepared for yourself?'

[21]"This is how it will be for those who store up things for themselves and are not rich toward God."

Luke 12:15-21

4. Describe the balance between preparing for the future financially and hoarding your wealth?

_____

_____

_____

_____

_____

5. What pressures in our society cause us to define ourselves by our possessions?

_____

_____

_____

_____

_____

6. In what ways do we demonstrate a lack of trust in God's provision for our needs?

_____

_____

_____

_____

_____

_____

More from the Word

44 ²⁷Consider how the lilies grow; they don't work or make clothes for themselves. But I tell you that even Solomon with his riches was not dressed as beautifully as one of these flowers. ²⁸God clothes the grass in the field, which is alive today but tomorrow is thrown into the fire. So how much more will God clothe you? Don't have so little faith!²⁹Don't always think about what you will eat or what you will drink, and don't keep worrying. ³⁰All the people in the world are trying to get these things, and your Father knows you need them. ³¹But seek God's kingdom, and all the other things you need will be given to you.

Luke 12:27-31

7. How does greed show itself even in the necessities of life like food and clothing?

_____

_____

_____

_____

_____

8. What does it mean to "seek God's kingdom"?

_____

_____

_____

_____

_____

_____

_____

9. Besides the price we pay for our possessions, what price do we pay in life for our greed?

_____

_____

_____

_____

_____

_____

_____

_____

My Reflections

"Greed is relative. Greed is not defined by what something costs; it is measured by what it costs you. If anything costs you your faith or your family, the price is too high." —Max

Journal

Which of my possessions are the most important to me and would be the hardest for me to let go?

_____

_____

_____

_____

_____

_____

_____

_____

_____

_____

_____

_____

_____

_____

_____

_____

_____

For Further Study

To study more about greed, read Proverbs 15:27; Proverbs 28:25; 1 Corinthians 6:9-11; Ephesians 5:3-5; Colossians 3:5; 1 Timothy 6:10; Hebrews 13:5; 1 John 3:17.

Additional Questions

10. Describe the biblical balance between welath and stewardship.

_____

_____

_____

_____

_____

_____

11. At what age do you think we start learning to define ourselves by the things we own or have?

_____

_____

_____

_____

_____

_____

12. How do you respond to the phrase, "Everybody has his price"?

_____

_____

_____

_____

_____

_____

Additional Thoughts

_____

_____

_____

_____

_____

_____

_____

_____

_____

_____

_____

The Choice

*"**F**or the next twelve hours I will be exposed to the day's demands. It is now that I must make a choice. Because of Calvary, I'm free to choose. And so I choose."* —Max Lucado

1. What helps you begin your day with a good attitude?

_____

_____

_____

_____

_____

_____

_____

A Moment with Max

Max shares these insights with us in his book *When God Whispers Your Name*.

I choose love…

No occasion justifies hatred; no injustice warrants bitterness. I choose love. Today I will love God and what God loves.

I choose joy…

I will invite my God to be the God of circumstance.

I choose peace…

I will live forgiven. I will forgive so that I may live.

I choose patience…

I will overlook the inconveniences of the world. Instead of cursing the one who takes my place, I'll invite him to do so.

I choose kindness…

I will be kind to the poor, for they are alone. Kind to the rich, for they are afraid. And kind to the unkind, for such is how God has treated me.

I choose goodness…

I will go without a dollar before I take a dishonest one.

I choose faithfulness…

Today I will keep my promises.

I choose gentleness…

Nothing is won by force. I choose to be gentle.

I choose self-control…

I refuse to let what will rot, rule the eternal…I will be drunk only by joy.

2. On a scale of 1 to 10 (1 being easy and 10 being difficult), how hard is it for you to maintain a positive attitude on a daily basis?

_____

_____

_____

_____

3. What three choices would make the world a better place if every person made those choices each morning?

_____

_____

A Message from the Word

²¹I know that you heard about him, and you are in him, so you were taught the truth that is in Jesus. ²²You were taught to leave your old self—to stop living the evil way you lived before. That old self becomes worse, because people are fooled by the evil things they want to do. ²³But you were taught to be made new in your hearts, ²⁴to become a new person. That new person is made to be like God—made to be truly good and holy.

²⁵So you must stop telling lies. Tell each other the truth, because we all belong to each other in the same body. ²⁶When you are angry, do not sin, and be sure to stop being angry before the end of the day. ²⁷Do not give the devil a way to defeat you. ²⁸Those who are stealing must stop stealing and start working. They should earn an honest living for themselves. Then they will have something to share with those who are poor.

²⁹When you talk, do not say harmful things, but say what people need—words that will help others become stronger. Then what you say will do good to those who listen to you. ³⁰And do not make the Holy Spirit sad. The Spirit is God's proof that you belong to him. God gave you the Spirit to show that God will make you free when the final day comes. ³¹Do not be bitter or angry or mad. Never shout angrily or say things to hurt others. Never do anything evil. ³²Be kind and loving to each other, and forgive each other just as God forgave you in Christ.

¹You are God's children whom he loves, so try to be like him. ²Live a life of love just as Christ loved us and gave himself for us as a sweet-smelling offering and sacrifice to God.

Ephesians 4:21—5:2

4. To live the kind of life described in this passage, what kind of choices would you have to make every day?

5. How did Jesus exemplify the attitudes described in this Scripture?

_____

_____

_____

_____

_____

6. What attitudes often stand in the way of living a life of love?

_____

_____

_____

_____

_____

_____

More from the Word

[5]In your lives you must think and act like Christ Jesus.
[6]Christ himself was like God in everything.
   But he did not think that being equal with God was something to be used for his own benefit.
[7]But he gave up his place with God and made himself nothing.

He was born to be a man
and became like a servant.
⁸And when he was living as a man,
he humbled himself and was fully obedient to God,
even when that caused his death—death on a cross.

Philippians 2:5-8

7. What words would you use to describe Christ's attitude while he lived on earth?

_____

_____

_____

_____

_____

8. How does your choice of attitude at the beginning of the day affect the remainder of it?

_____

_____

_____

_____

_____

9. In your own words, what does it mean to have a servant attitude?

_____

_____

_____

_____

_____

My Reflections

"Love, joy, peace, patience, kindness, goodness, faithfulness, gentleness, and self-control. To these I commit my day. If I succeed, I will give thanks. If I fail, I will seek his grace. And then, when this day is done, I will place my head on my pillow and rest." —Max

Journal

I would like to see more of these attitudes in my life:

_____

_____

_____

_____

_____

_____

_____

_____

_____

_____

_____

For Further Study

To study more about spiritual attitudes, read Psalm 86:11; Matthew 3:8; Romans 8:5-10, 12-17; 1 Corinthians 2:11-16; Galatians 5:22-26; Ephesians 6:10-18; Colossians 3:5-10, 12-17.

Additional Questions

10. What is God's attitude toward us?

_____

_____

_____

_____

_____

_____

11. What spiritual attitudes are the most difficult for you to maintain?

_____

_____

_____

_____

_____

_____

12. When did someone else's attitude make all the difference for you?

_____

_____

_____

_____

_____

_____

Additional Thoughts

_____

_____

_____

_____

_____

_____

_____

_____

_____

_____

_____

_____

_____

Vengeance Is Whose?

"Revenge belongs to God! If vengeance is God's then it is not ours. God has not asked us to settle the score or get even. Ever. Judgment is God's job. To assume otherwise is to assume God can't do it." —Max Lucado

1. Describe a situation from your childhood when you wanted to get even with someone.

_____

_____

_____

_____

_____

_____

_____

_____

A Moment with Max

Max shares these insights with us in his book *When God Whispers Your Name*.

Anger has a way of increasing in volume until it's the only sound we hear. The louder it gets the more desperate we become.

When we are mistreated, our animalistic response is to go on the hunt. Instinctively, we double up our fists. Getting even is only natural. Which, incidentally, is precisely the problem. Revenge is natural, not spiritual. Getting even is the rule of the jungle. Giving grace is the rule of the kingdom.

X-ray the soul of the vengeful and behold the tumor of bitterness: black, menacing, malignant. Carcinoma of the spirit. Its fatal fibers creep around the edge of the heart and ravage it. Yesterday you can't alter, but your reaction to yesterday you can. The past you cannot change, but your response to the past you can.

2. If left unchecked, how can anger and a thirst for revenge destroy a person's life?

_____

_____

_____

_____

_____

_____

A Message from the Word

[27]"But I say to you who are listening, love your enemies. Do good to those who hate you, [28]bless those who curse you, pray for those who are cruel to you. [29]If anyone slaps you on one cheek, offer him the other cheek, too. If someone takes your coat, do not stop him from taking your shirt. [30]Give to everyone who asks you, and when someone takes something that is yours,

don't ask for it back. [31]Do to others what you would want them to do to you. [32]If you love only the people who love you, what praise should you get? Even sinners love the people who love them. [33]If you do good only to those who do good to you, what praise should you get? Even sinners do that![34]If you lend things to people, always hoping to get something back, what praise should you get? Even sinners lend to other sinners so that they can get back the same amount![35]But love your enemies, do good to them, and lend to them without hoping to get anything back. Then you will have a great reward, and you will be children of the Most High God, because he is kind even to people who are ungrateful and full of sin. [36]Show mercy, just as your Father shows mercy.

Luke 6:27-36

3. What motivates people to hold grudges against others?

_____

_____

_____

_____ 63

_____

_____

_____

4. According to this Scripture, what's in store for those who do good to those who hurt them?

_____

_____

_____

_____

_____

_____

_____

5. What is the balance between rightfully defending yourself and seeking revenge?

_____

_____

_____

_____

_____

_____

More from the Word

64   ¹⁷If someone does wrong to you, do not pay him back by doing wrong to him. Try to do what everyone thinks is right. ¹⁸Do your best to live in peace with everyone. ¹⁹My friends, do not try to punish others when they wrong you, but wait for God to punish them with his anger. It is written: "I will punish those who do wrong; I will repay them," says the Lord. ²⁰But you should do this:
    "If your enemy is hungry, feed him;
    if he is thirsty, give him a drink.
    Doing this will be like pouring burning coals on his head."
²¹Do not let evil defeat you, but defeat evil by doing good.

Romans 12:17–21

6. What makes us believe it is possible to defeat evil by doing good?

_____

_____

_____

_____

_____

7. How much of our desire for revenge is really a sense of justice?

_____

_____

_____

_____

_____

8. In what circumstances is it right and good to seek justice?

_____

_____

_____

_____

_____

My Reflections

"Revenge is irreverent. When we strike back we are saying, 'I know vengeance is yours, God, but I just didn't think you'd punish enough. I thought I'd better take this situation into my own hands. You have a tendency to be a little soft.'

"...To forgive someone is to display reverence. Forgiveness is not saying the one who hurt you was right. Forgiveness is stating that God is fair and he will do what is right.

"After all, don't we have enough things to do without trying to do God's work too?" —Max

Journal

In what situation or relationship in my life am I still holding out for some revenge?

For Further Study

To study more about revenge, read Leviticus 19:17-18; Psalm 18:17-24; Psalm 108:12-13; Proverbs 24:15-20; Matthew 5:10-12, 38-47; 1 Peter 2:21-24.

Additional Questions

9. How does anger affect us physically and emotionally?

_____

_____

_____

_____

_____

_____

_____

_____

10. How does it feel to let go of hurts or injustices you've suffered?

_____

_____

_____

_____

_____

_____

_____

11. How do others typically respond when you repay evil with good?

_____

_____

_____

_____

_____

Additional Thoughts

_____

_____

_____

_____

_____

_____

_____

_____

_____

_____

_____

_____

_____

Geronimo!

"I stand a few feet from the mirror and see the face of a man who failed ... I promised I wouldn't but I did. If this were the first time, it would be different. But it isn't. How many times can one fall and expect to be caught?"
—Max Lucado

1. Describe a time when you experienced God's protection in an amazing way.

_____

_____

_____

_____

_____

_____

_____

A Moment with Max

Max shares these insights with us in his book *When God Whispers Your Name*.

I stand six steps from the bed's edge. My arms extended. Hands open. On the bed Sara - all four years of her—crouches, posed like a playful kitten. She's going to jump. But she's not ready. I'm too close.

"Back more, Daddy," she stands and dares.

...Once again she crouches, then springs. Superman without a cape. Skydiver without a chute. Only her heart flies higher than her body. In that airborne instant her only hope is her father. If he proves weak, she'll fall. If he proves cruel, she'll crash. If he proves forgetful, she'll tumble to the hard floor.

But such fear she does not know, for her father she does. She trusts him. Four years under the same roof have convinced her he is reliable. He is not superhuman, but he is strong. He is not holy, but he is good. He's not brilliant, but he doesn't have to be reminded to catch his child when she jumps.

And so she flies.

And so she soars.

And so he catches her and the two rejoice at the wedding of her trust and his faithfulness.

72

2. What is it about life that sometimes undermines our sense of childlike trust?

_____

_____

_____

_____

3. What makes us believe that we can take better care of ourselves than God can?

_____

_____

_____

_____

A Message from the Word

[35]Can anything separate us from the love Christ has for us? Can troubles or problems or sufferings or hunger or nakedness or danger or violent death?[36]As it is written in the Scriptures:

"For you we are in danger of death all the time.

People think we are worth no more than sheep to be killed."

[37]But in all these things we have full victory through God who showed his love for us. [38]Yes, I am sure that neither death, nor life, nor angels, nor ruling spirits, nothing now, nothing in the future, no powers, [39]nothing above us, nothing below us, nor anything else in the whole world will ever be able to separate us from the love of God that is in Christ Jesus our Lord.

Romans 8:35-39

4. When in your life did God seem far away?

_____

_____

_____

_____

_____

5. If God is always with us, what hinders us from feeling his presence in a tangible way?

_____

_____

_____

_____

_____

6. In practical terms, what does it mean for us that we can never be separated from God's love?

_____

_____

_____

_____

_____

_____

More from the Word

74   ¹⁵My eyes are always looking to the Lord for help.
    He will keep me from any traps.
  ¹⁶Turn to me and have mercy on me,
    because I am lonely and hurting.
  ¹⁷My troubles have grown larger;
    free me from my problems.
  ¹⁸Look at my suffering and troubles,
    and take away all my sins.
  ¹⁹Look at how many enemies I have!
    See how much they hate me!
  ²⁰Protect me and save me.
    I trust you, so do not let me be disgraced.
  ²¹My hope is in you,
    so may goodness and honesty guard me.

Psalm 25:15-21

7. What are some of the troubles you have faced?

_____

_____

_____

_____

_____

8. What kind of refuge is God in the midst of life's troubles?

_____

_____

_____

_____

_____

9. How does obeying God and living a life of integrity protect us?

_____ 75

_____

_____

_____

_____

My Reflections

" 'God's power is very great for us who believe,' Paul taught. 'That power is the same as the great strength God used to raise Christ from the dead' (Ephesians 1:19-20) Next time you wonder if God can catch you, read that verse. The very arms that defeated death are the arms awaiting you. Next time you wonder if God can forgive you, read that verse. The very hands that were nailed to the cross are open for you." —Max

Journal

In what area of my life do I need to trust God more fully?

_____

_____

_____

_____

_____

_____

_____

_____

_____

_____

_____

_____

_____

_____

_____

For Further Study

To study more about God's protection, read Psalm 5:11-12; Psalm 12:5-7; Psalm 32:6-7; Psalm 77:14-15; Psalm 91:14-16; Proverbs 2:6-8.

Additional Questions

10. What does it feel like when someone breaks your trust?

_____

_____

_____

_____

_____

11. How would you try to persuade another person of God's trustworthiness?

_____

_____

_____

_____

_____

_____

12. In what ways has God proven his trustworthiness to you in the past?

_____

_____

_____

_____

_____

_____

Additional Thoughts

_____

_____

_____

_____

_____

_____

_____

_____

_____

_____

_____

_____

_____

How Does God Spell "Relief"?

"It's hard to be affirming when you are affirmation-starved. It's hard to be forgiving when you feel guilty." —Max Lucado

1. How does your best friend's mood affect the way your day goes?

_____

_____

_____

_____

_____

_____

_____

_____

A Moment with Max

Max shares these insights with us in his book *When God Whispers Your Name*.

Paul had an interesting observation about the way we treat people. He said it about marriage, but the principle applies in any relationship. "The man who loves his wife loves himself" (Ephesians 5:28). There is a correlation between the way you feel about yourself and the way you feel about others. If you are at peace with yourself—if you like yourself—you will get along with others.

The converse is also true. If you don't like yourself, if you are ashamed, embarrassed, or angry, other people are going to know it. ...Which takes us to the question, "How *does* a person get relief?"

Which, in turn, takes us to one of the kindest verses in the Bible, "Come to me, all of you who are tired and have heavy loads, and I will give you rest. Accept my teachings and learn from me, because I am gentle and humble in spirit, and you will find rest for your lives. The teaching I ask you to accept is easy; the load I give you to carry is light" (Matthew 11:28-29).

You knew I was going to say that. I can see you holding this book and shaking your head. "I've tried that. I've read the Bible, I've sat on the pew—but I've never received relief."

If that is the case, could I ask a delicate but deliberate question? Could it be that you went to religion and didn't go to God? Could it be that you went to a church, but never saw Christ?

2. Why do you think some people do not find a sense of peace and rest in the church?

_____

_____

_____

_____

3. What kind of relief do you believe God wants you to have in this life?

_____

_____

_____

_____

A Message from the Word

²⁸Surely you know.
Surely you have heard.
The LORD is the God who lives forever,
who created all the world.
He does not become tired or need to rest.
No one can understand how great his wisdom is.
²⁹He gives strength to those who are tired
and more power to those who are weak.
³⁰Even children become tired and need to rest,
and young people trip and fall.
³¹But the people who trust the LORD will become strong again.
They will rise up as an eagle in the sky;
they will run and not need rest;
they will walk and not become tired.

Isaiah 40:28-31

4. What hope do these verses offer the discouraged and downhearted?

_____

_____

_____

_____

_____

5. What kinds of circumstances in life take the wind out of a person's sails?

_____

_____

_____

_____

_____

6. What can we learn from Jesus' example about finding relief from the struggles of life?

_____

_____

_____

_____

_____

_____

More from the Word

¹⁴Since we have a great high priest, Jesus the Son of God, who has gone into heaven, let us hold on to the faith we have. ¹⁵For our high priest is able to understand our weaknesses. When he lived on earth, he was tempted in every way that we are, but he did not sin. ¹⁶Let us, then, feel very sure that we can come before God's throne where there is grace. There we can receive mercy and grace to help us when we need it.

Hebrews 4:14–16

7. How does knowing that Christ himself faced temptations and struggles help you in your difficult times?

_____

_____

_____

_____

_____

8. What are some reasons that you might approach God's throne without confidence?

_____

_____

_____

_____

_____

_____

_____

9. What usually keeps you from turning to God and trusting him for help?

_____

_____

_____

_____

_____

_____

_____

My Reflections

"Jesus says he is the solution for weariness of soul. Go to him. Be honest with him. Admit you have soul secrets you've never dealt with. He already knows what they are. He's just waiting for you to ask him to help."

—Max

Journal

How can I depend on God to help me deal with the things in my life that are weighing me down?

For Further Study

To study more about God's comfort and relief, read Psalm 4:1; Psalm 16:5-11; Psalm 23:1-4; Psalm 62:1-2; Psalm 119:50; Isaiah 30:15-18.

Additional Questions

10. What was the most restful and renewing experience you've ever had?

_____

_____

_____

_____

_____

_____

11. How do you approach the world when you are feeling rejected?

_____

_____

_____

_____

_____

_____

_____

12. If regret was something you could measure, what kinds of regrets do you think would be the biggest?

_____

_____

_____

_____

_____

_____

Additional Thoughts

_____

_____

_____

_____

_____

_____

_____

_____

_____

_____

_____

There's No Place Like Home

"The moral of The Wizard of Oz*? Everything you may need, you've already got. The power you need is really a power you already have. Just look deep enough, long enough, and there's nothing you can't do. Sound familiar? Sound patriotic? Sound Christian?" —Max Lucado*

1. From what other sources do we hear the message, "Everything you need is within yourself"?

_____

_____

_____

_____

_____

_____

_____

_____

A Moment with Max

Max shares these insights with us in his book *When God Whispers Your Name*.

Do-it-yourself Christianity is not much encouragement to the done in and worn out.

Self-sanctification holds little hope for the addict.

"Try a little harder" is little encouragement for the abused.

At some point we need more than good advice; we need help. Somewhere on this journey home we realize that a fifty-fifty proposition is too little. We need more—more than a pudgy wizard who thanks us for coming but tells us the trip was unnecessary.

We need help. Help from the inside out. The kind of help Jesus promised. "I will ask the Father, and he will give you another Helper to be with you forever—the Spirit of truth. The world cannot accept him, because it does not see him or know him. But you know him, because he lives with you and will be *in* you" (John 14:16–17, emphasis mine).

Note the final words of the verse. And in doing so, note the dwelling place of God—"in you."

Not near us. Not above us. Not around us. But in us. In the part of us we don't even know. In the heart no one else has seen. In the hidden recesses of our being dwells, not an angel, not a philosophy, not a genie, but God.

Imagine that.

2. When did you first become aware of God's presence in you?

_____

_____

_____

_____

3. How would you describe to an unbeliever the difference God's presence makes in your everyday life?

_____

_____

_____

_____

A Message from the Word

⁶If people's thinking is controlled by the sinful self, there is death. But if their thinking is controlled by the Spirit, there is life and peace. ⁷When people's thinking is controlled by the sinful self, they are against God, because they refuse to obey God's law and really are not even able to obey God's law. ⁸Those people who are ruled by their sinful selves cannot please God.

⁹But you are not ruled by your sinful selves. You are ruled by the Spirit, if that Spirit of God really lives in you. But the person who does not have the Spirit of Christ does not belong to Christ. ¹⁰Your body will always be dead because of sin. But if Christ is in you, then the Spirit gives you life, because Christ made you right with God. ¹¹God raised Jesus from the dead, and if God's Spirit is living in you, he will also give life to your bodies that die. God is the One who raised Christ from the dead, and he will give life through his Spirit that lives in you.

Romans 8:6–11

4. According to this passage, how can people find life and peace?

_____

_____

_____

_____

_____

5. What does it mean to be ruled by the Spirit?

_____

_____

_____

_____

6. What responsibilities come with being a dwelling place for God's Spirit?

_____

_____

_____

_____

_____

More from the Word

94 [16]Don't you know that you are God's temple and that God's Spirit lives in you?[17]If anyone destroys God's temple, God will destroy that person, because God's temple is holy and you are that temple.

[18]Do not fool yourselves. If you think you are wise in this world, you should become a fool so that you can become truly wise, [19]because the wisdom of this world is foolishness with God. It is written in the Scriptures, "He catches those who are wise in their own clever traps."[20]It is also written in the Scriptures, "The Lord knows what wise people think. He knows their thoughts are just a puff of wind."

1 Corinthians 3:16–20

7. In what ways can we destroy God's dwelling place within us?

_____

_____

_____

_____

_____

_____

8. How does the wisdom of our culture teach us to look to self rather than God?

_____

_____

_____

_____

_____

_____

9. How can we listen to the Spirit dwelling within us?

_____

_____

_____

_____

_____

_____

_____

My Reflections

" 'Do you not know,' Paul penned, 'that your body is the temple of the Holy Spirit?' (1 Corinthians 6:19 NKJV). Perhaps you didn't. Perhaps you didn't know God would go that far to make sure you got home. If not, thanks for letting me remind you. The wizard says look inside yourself and find self. God says look inside yourself and find God. The first will get you to Kansas. The latter will get you to heaven. Take your pick." —Max

Journal

In what tangible way can I embrace God's presence in my life?

_____

_____

_____

_____

_____

_____

_____

_____

_____

_____

_____

_____

_____

_____

_____

_____

For Further Study

To study more about God's indwelling presence, read John 14:23; Romans 8:11; Galatians 3:1-11; Ephesians 2:8-10; Philippians 2:12-13; Colossians 1:27.

Additional Questions

10. How is becoming a Christian like coming home?

_____

_____

_____

_____

_____

_____

11.What was the biggest change you saw in yourself after you became a Christian?

_____

_____

_____

_____

_____

_____

12. Describe God's presence in your life and what it means to you.

_____

_____

_____

_____

_____

_____

Additional Thoughts

_____

_____

_____

_____

_____

_____

_____

_____

_____

_____

_____

_____

Warning! Warning!

"Spray paint won't fix rust.
A Band-Aid™ won't remove a tumor.
Wax on the hood won't cure the cough of a
motor. If the problem is inside, you have to go
inside." —Max Lucado

1. List some things that can look good on the out-side but be rotten on the inside.

_____

_____

_____

_____

_____

_____

_____

A Moment with Max

Max shares these insights with us in his book *When God Whispers Your Name*.

Alarms sound in your world...Maybe not with bells and horns, but with problems and pain. Their purpose is to signal impending danger. A fit of anger is a red flare. Uncontrolled debt is a flashing light. A guilty conscience is a warning sign indicating trouble within. Icy relationships are posted notices announcing anything from neglect to abuse.

You have alarms in your life. When they go off, how do you respond? Be honest now. Hasn't there been a time or two when you went outside for a solution when you should have gone inward?

Ever blamed your plight on Washington? (If they'd lower the tax rates, my business would work.) Inculpated your family for your failure? (Mom always liked my sister more.) Called God to account for your problems? (If he is God, why doesn't he heal my marriage?) Faulted the church for your frail faith? (Those people are a bunch of hypocrites.)

Your circumstances may be challenging, but blaming them is not the solution. Nor is neglecting them. Heaven knows you don't silence life's alarms by pretending they aren't screaming. But heaven also knows it's wise to look in the mirror before you peek out the window.

Consider the prayer of David: "Create *in* me a pure heart, O God, and renew a steadfast spirit *within* me" (Psalm 51:10 NIV).

2. What warning signs tell us something is wrong with us physically?

_____

_____

_____

_____

3. What are the warning signs that tell us something is wrong with us spiritually?

_____

_____

_____

_____

A Message from the Word

[15]I do not understand the things I do. I do not do what I want to do, and I do the things I hate. [16]And if I do not want to do the hated things I do, that means I agree that the law is good. [17]But I am not really the one who is doing these hated things; it is sin living in me that does them. [18]Yes, I know that nothing good lives in me—I mean nothing good lives in the part of me that is earthly and sinful. I want to do the things that are good, but I do not do them. [19]I do not do the good things I want to do, but I do the bad things I do not want to do. [20]So if I do things I do not want to do, then I am not the one doing them. It is sin living in me that does those things.

[21]So I have learned this rule: When I want to do good, evil is there with me. [22]In my mind, I am happy with God's law. [23]But I see another law working in my body, which makes war against the law that my mind accepts. That other law working in my body is the law of sin, and it makes me its prisoner. [24]What a miserable man I am! Who will save me from this body that brings me death? [25]I thank God for saving me through Jesus Christ our Lord!

So in my mind I am a slave to God's law, but in my sinful self I am a slave to the law of sin.

Romans 7:15–25

4. How do you explain why we do what we hate and don't do what we want to do?

_____

_____

_____

_____

_____

5. What "other law" is working against us?

_____

_____

_____

_____

_____

6. How can we escape the clutches of sin?

_____

_____

_____

_____

_____

More from the Word

³When I kept things to myself,
  I felt weak deep inside me.
  I moaned all day long.
⁴Day and night you punished me.
  My strength was gone as in the summer heat. Selah
⁵Then I confessed my sins to you
  and didn't hide my guilt.
I said, "I will confess my sins to the LORD,"
  and you forgave my guilt. Selah

Psalm 32:3-5

7. What red flags in your life stir you to seek God's forgiveness?

_____

_____

_____

_____

8. What does it mean to be forgiven and restored to a right relationship with God and others?

_____

_____

_____

_____

_____

_____

9. If forgiveness is there for the asking, why do we sometimes hesitate to seek and accept it?

_____

_____

_____

_____

_____

_____

My Reflections

"The next time alarms go off in your world, ask yourself three questions.
  1. Is there any unconfessed sin in my life?
  2. Are there any unresolved conflicts in my world?
  3. Are there any unsurrendered worries in my heart?
Alarms serve a purpose. They signal a problem. Sometimes the problem is *out there*. More often it's *in here*. So before you peek outside, take a good look inside." —Max

Journal

What warning signals in my life are telling me to take time to look inside?

_____

_____

_____

_____

_____

_____

_____

_____

_____

_____

_____

_____

_____

_____

_____

For Further Study

To study more about sin, read Psalm 32:1-2; Psalm 36:1-4; Psalm 38:5-18; Ecclesiastes 7:20; Isaiah 1:18-20; Hosea 14:1-2; Matthew 23:25-28; Mark 7:20-23; Romans 8:1-11; Colossians 2:13-15.

Additional Questions

10. How does sin creep into our lives at times without our noticing?

_____

_____

_____

_____

_____

11. How do unresolved conflicts affect us?

_____

_____

_____

_____

_____

_____

12. How do you surrender a worry that is in your heart?

_____

_____

_____

_____

_____

_____

_____

Additional Thoughts

_____

_____

_____

_____

_____

_____

_____

_____

_____

_____

Healthy Habits

"I like the story of the little boy who fell out of bed. When his Mom asked him what happened, he answered, 'I don't know. I guess I stayed too close to where I got in.' Easy to do the same with our faith. It's tempting just to stay where we got in and never move." —Max Lucado

1. In your opinion, what are the two hardest habits to change?

_____

_____

_____

_____

_____

_____

_____

_____

A Moment with Max

Max shares these insights with us in his book *When God Whispers Your Name*.

Growth is the goal of the Christian. Maturity is mandatory. If a child ceased to develop, the parent would be concerned, right? Doctors would be called. Tests would be run. When a child stops growing, something is wrong.

When a Christian stops growing, help is needed. If you are the same Christian you were a few months ago, be careful. You might be wise to get a checkup. Not on your body, but on your heart. Not a physical, but a spiritual.

May I suggest one?

First the habit of prayer: "Base your happiness on your hope in Christ. When trials come endure them patiently; steadfastly maintain the habit of prayer" (Romans 12:12 PHILLIPS).

Second, the habit of study: "The man who looks into the perfect law…and makes a habit of so doing, is not the man who sees and forgets. He puts that law into practice and he wins true happiness" (James 1:25 PHILLIPS).

Third, the habit of giving: "Every Sunday each of you should put aside something from what you have earned during the week, and use it for this offering. The amount depends on how much the Lord has helped you earn" (1 Corinthians 16:2 TLB).

And last of all, the habit of fellowship: "Let us not give up the habit of meeting together, as some are doing. Instead let us encourage one another" (Hebrews 10:25 TEV).

2. What are the three spiritual habits that you feel most strengthen your walk with God?

_____

_____

_____

_____

3. What often hinders us from developing new habits that will help us grow spiritually?

_____

_____

_____

A Message from the Word

⁴⁷I will show you what everyone is like who comes to me and hears my words and obeys. ⁴⁸That person is like a man building a house who dug deep and laid the foundation on rock. When the floods came, the water tried to wash the house away, but it could not shake it, because the house was built well. ⁴⁹But the one who hears my words and does not obey is like a man who built his house on the ground without a foundation. When the floods came, the house quickly fell and was completely destroyed."

Luke 6:47–49

4. How do good spiritual habits function like a good foundation?

_____

_____

_____

_____

_____

_____

5. Describe the joy that is found in obeying God's commands.

_____

_____

_____

_____

_____

_____

_____

6. What results when we fail to obey God's commands?

_____

_____

_____

_____

_____

More from the Word

⁵⁴I sing about your demands
   wherever I live.
⁵⁵LORD, I remember you at night,
   and I will obey your teachings.
⁵⁶This is what I do:
   I follow your orders.
⁵⁷LORD, you are my share in life;
   I have promised to obey your words.
⁵⁸I prayed to you with all my heart.
   Have mercy on me as you have promised.
⁵⁹I thought about my life,
   and I decided to follow your rules.
⁶⁰I hurried and did not wait
   to obey your commands.

Psalm 119:54-60

7. What part does self-examination play in changing life habits?

_____

_____

_____

_____

_____

_____

8. What happens when we obey God out of habit?

_____

_____

_____

_____

_____

9. How do we relate to God differently when we are in the habit of obeying him?

_____

_____

_____

_____

_____

My Reflections

"There they are … habits worth having. Isn't it good to know that some habits are good for you? Make them a part of your day and grow. Don't make the mistake of the little boy. Don't stay too close to where you got in. It's risky resting on the edge." —Max

Journal

A year from now, what new habits would I like to have incorporated into my life?

For Further Study

To study more about developing godly habits, read Proverbs 15:32; Matthew 7:24-27; Philippians 4:8-9; 2 Timothy 1:7; Titus 1:6-9.

Additional Questions

10. What does it take to form a new habit?

_____

_____

_____

_____

_____

_____

_____

11. What does it take to change an old habit?

_____

_____

_____

_____

_____

_____

12. Describe someone who, in your estimation, maintains a lifestyle of godly habits. What can you learn from that person?

_____

_____

_____

_____

_____

_____

Additional Thoughts

_____

_____

_____

_____

_____

_____

_____

_____

_____

_____